Butterfly in a Jar

Kimberly Raven

DEDICATION

I dedicate this book to my mother and bestie the late Mrs. Margaret Raven who was and still is my inspiration and will always remain my biggest supporter. My mother exemplified the true definition of a humanitarian. She dedicated her life to her family, friends and educating within the Public School System. My mother loved unconditionally, served unselfishly, encouraged consistently, and supported me in all my endeavors until the day she was called home. She left a legacy of love, fire, and desire within me to spread my wings and soar like the Raven that I am.

Special Heavenly Dedication to my father Jesse Raven, my aunt Annie Lee Dixon, and my aunt Geraldine Strong. Love & Miss You

BUTTERFLY IN A JAR

Table of Contents

Dedication

Special Heavenly Dedication

Acknowledgement

BUTTERFLY IN A JAR

Acknowledgement

I would like to acknowledge the inspirational people in my life. First honor to God for being the head of my life, for your love, mercy, and grace. Sending hugs and kisses to my heavenly parents Jesse and Margaret Raven, THANK YOU! for life and loving me unconditionally. I miss you dearly. Sending love to my two sons Darius and DeAnthony you are my life and inspiration in everything that I do and that I am, I love YOU and I'm proud to be your Mom. Thank you to my cousins Wanda and Morineke for always checking up on me and supporting me. Sending love to my publisher and friend LaQuita Parks of Pa-Pro-Vi publishing for your honesty, guidance, words of wisdom and the girl talks. Sending love and hugs for your continued support to my organizations The Dirtybirds Squad and The MasterMINDZ. I cannot end this acknowledgement without showing love to my hometown the City of Atlanta and the alumni of my high school Walter F. George High School. Thank you for your encouraging words, love, and support. You all have helped create this butterfly and now it's time for me to fly. I LOVE YOU ALL!!

FORWARD

There are those who go through life with a smile, often real but most times fake; however, some smiles are cover-ups for the real wounds of life. Sometimes the smile serves to cover a crisis that silenced them.

Life is about change that may be necessary to assist us with emerging from our cocoon of wounds. This book serves to highlight the metamorphosis of the author. The content of the book will enlighten you as you allow the context of the content to move you through her life. Just as a caterpillar must struggle through the bevy of stages to emerge different from the struggle, humans are faced with struggles.

The author will guide the readers through the different stages of her transformation. She will engage, enlighten, and encourage the readers to move from a crawling worm in the dust of the vicissitudes of life, to soar above a lowly beginning.

I am honored to present to you, Kimberly Raven's, Butterfly in a Jar.

LaQuita Parks

"To become a Butterfly, you must first digest yourself."

INTRODUCTION

Butterfly In a Jar is about how I lost myself within the cracks of life and how taking control back over my life through life altering transformation allowed me to fly. We can all relate and reflect at some point in our lives feeling stagnated and losing ourselves in the process. You start to have those agitating feelings of not being in control of your life, so you look for ways to pass the time, cover the hurt and hide the scars. Your emotions grab you and take you on a roller coaster ride of anxiety, fear, isolation, and rejection. You feel alone, then depression set in and your mind starts to play tricks on you to the point of no return. When enough is enough and you feel as though you're about to lose all consciousness.... you take a *deep sigh* and make up your mind that it's time to radically transform your mind, body and soul and fly.

Believe in yourself and know that you deserve all the great things that the universe will serve you. Growth does not come without the pain of truth and YOUR TRUTH will set you free. Don't be afraid to digest yourself, learn yourself, forgive yourself and reinvent yourself into something beautiful. Just like a butterfly grows through the beautiful stages of life, we too, grow through the stages of life to become our beautiful and unique selves.

"We delight in the beauty of the butterfly, but rarely admit the changes it has gone through to achieve that beauty" ~Maya Angelou~

Chapter 1

Beginning of my *Butterfly* Process

"Our lives are shaped by our experiences and the passage of time. It's in that time that we are delicate with life trials and tribulations and must digest ourselves and search our souls to be ready to spread our wings. When you can look back at your past and want to be better and not bitter, YOU'VE WON!!"
~Kimberly Raven~

My life is no fairy tale but like the butterfly process, the different stages growing from childhood to adulthood have shaped and transformed my mental, spiritual, physical, and emotional well-being. I learned from my mother at an early age how to be strong, an independent thinker, outspoken, caretaker and courageous. I am the last child and only girl with two older brothers born on a cold winter's night on February 7, 1971, in Atlanta, Georgia to the parents of the late Jesse & Margaret Raven

I grew up in Southeast Atlanta, as a young girl in the community of Thomasville Heights. This is where my butterfly experience started. Early morning playtime on weekends with my friends was the best. We didn't have video games, cell phones or social media to grab our attention. All we needed to have a good time was each other, our own eccentric imaginations. It didn't matter to us what anybody had or didn't have. We just enjoyed playing together. I think of those times playing hopscotch, marbles, riding our bikes, catching lightning bugs, yellow bees, and going to the community pool, which is where I learned how to swim.

During my younger years when I was starting school in kindergarten, we attended school just a half a day, meaning that you either attended school in the morning sessions or the afternoon sessions. Being that my mother worked for the school system, I attended the morning sessions at school and my mom would come and pick me up on her break. I would spend the remainder of the day in her classroom playing with the other children, participating, and interacting in her class activities.

I attended the neighborhood school Thomasville Elementary School from kindergarten through fifth grade. I loved my school, my teachers, and friends. My brothers and I had complete advantage to the school as we lived right across the street from the school. Seriously, we could actually look out our door and see the school. There was absolutely no reason for us to be late, and tardiness and cutting up at school was definitely non-negotiable.

We attended church on a regular basis and I experienced my first baptism at an early age at Calvary Hill Baptist Church. I didn't quite grasp the reason for baptism at that young age, but in my later years I would come to love and understand Christianity and fall even more in love with Jesus that I recommitted myself to him in January 2020. It's funny you never fully understand some of the choices and decisions that you make or are made for you until some time has passed. Then you come up with all kinds of rewrites and replays in your mind of what you should have or could have done. I had to learn early how to speak up for myself, live for myself or else my wings would never grow and I would continue to stay nestled in silence. Once things change inside you, things start to change around you. A change was on the way once I entered middle School.

I was in a new location with new people which I felt were sometimes awkward. I didn't really adapt and open up in new environments, it took me a minute to break my shy code. But once I was comfortable around people I opened up more not only with my peers, but my teachers as well. I started to feel a little mature (so I thought) since I was attending school with eighth graders. My taste in friends changed, my interest in boys had my eyes wide open and wouldn't you know Mother Nature made her presence known too. This butterfly was definitely discovering herself and life as I knew was about to change.

CHAPTER 2

Life As I Knew It

"What seems like bitter trials are often

butterfly blessings in disguise"

I tried my best to bury my past deep within my subconscious mind. For years I had felt like a butterfly in a jar with only minimal air to breathe with no opportunity to fly. The more I gasped for air to breathe, the more my wings of determination to fly started to feel heavy and frustrated. To no avail, I submitted to the frustration of waiting on a miracle for change rather than choices to change. I simply went along with my everyday lifestyle with a smile on my face, all while my spirit was shattering on the inside.

During my adolescent years I found myself navigating through life with different emotions discovering my body and trying to figure out who I was meant to be. I was fantasizing and visualizing this amazing future but could barely breathe feeling like a butterfly in a jar. I knew there was a world of possibilities waiting to be released in my future. Isn't it weird to have love from your parents, friends and family and still feel alone? When things were changing inside of me mentally and emotionally and my homelife took a turn unexpectedly, I didn't lash out as most people would do at the sign of change. I nestled more within myself of self-isolation trying to figure things out on my own and hoped that things would get better.

During this time, my parents had separated due to my dad's alcoholism. It's no secret that anger and alcohol can dismantle a family. At times when my father would drink, his behavior and moods reminded me of the characters Dr. Jekyll and Mr. Hyde. In one way he could be nice, talkative, and even playful, singing to us and I loved seeing him dance with my mom as he replayed his favorite artists like Sam Cooke, The Temptations, The Drifters, and The Spinners. I clearly remember when he was in a good mood, he would love to tell me about the day I was born and how cold it was on that February day.

He could go on and on about how beautiful I was with a head full of hair and his laughter on how I was the only baby crying loudly disturbing the other babies in the nursery. He didn't know it, but no matter how old I got, on his good day I would look forward to him telling that story because I enjoyed seeing the glow in his eyes and seeing him smile when he expressed himself. I notice that he could only really express himself to us about some things that he was feeling emotionally when he was in a good mood and drinking.

On the other side of that glow his behavior changes and intensifies his mental capacity. There were several times that he was enraged, but one that stands out and affected me the most was the one night he was out drinking and came home in a rage and arguing with my mom. I didn't quite understand clearly what the argument was about but I do remember being awakened by my mom's voice yelling his name and telling him STOP!! STOP!! As she was in the bathroom cleaning the tub, she was trying to defend herself as my dad was yelling, hitting, and pulling her hair. Since this was an ongoing process when he drank, the arguing and yelling would subside shortly after he got home and the house would be calm and we can get some sleep, but on this particular night it just disturbed my soul to the point where for the first time I had to intervene.

At that moment hearing the desperation in my mom's voice, I had to do something because enough was enough for me. I was tired of living in this environment and was fed up with being scared and on eggshells. I had felt and heard rage in his voice before, but this time it felt different in my spirit that I was scared and I knew this time was not the time to just wait for it to be over. I jumped out of my bed, opened my bedroom door and the bathroom was right across from the room, I grabbed his arm distracting him from my mom and I was yelling at him "Dad STOP!! STOP!! Leave her alone!" I didn't know what to expect in response to my actions, but I had no idea what would come next and I didn't care, I was just tired!!!

My dad was so furious that one of his children had stood up to him that without thinking, he lashed out at me and swung on me, but I was too quick and ducked so I missed the connection of his fist to my face but I took a hit on my arm all while he was yelling and cursing at me hurtful words. My mom intervened to make him stop and to make sure I was okay. Something came over me and I was proud of myself for finally standing up to this behavior and some part of me lost respect for him and suppressed bitterness and anger within myself. It changed my outlook on men and relationships. It was a lesson for me as to what Kim was and was not going to accept in my future relationships, It changed my relationship with my dad and I became distant and really didn't care if I spoke to him again. I needed time to digest what had happened and space to think.

I was in high school at the time and had to figure out how to not wear my hurt and anger on my sleeve and keep it moving so no one would know what I was dealing with behind closed doors. As I got older things got better between us where I could be in the same room but I refused to live with him in the same household again. As I look back now and finding out more about my dad's upbringing, I know that his behavior was not intentional but a form of depression and drinking was his coping mechanism. Depression is real and it is a big part of a families' demise in connecting with one another, I only wish that it was recognized earlier and that it could have been addressed as a family. I know my dad loved my mom and his children, If only he could have looked in the mirror and loved what he saw and got the help he needed, I think our family could have been saved from the Jekyll-and-Hyde behavior.

I was born into that life and I can admit today that I was embarrassed and ashamed of people knowing that family secret. I walked on eggshells most of the time because you didn't know if or when he would go into a rant. Most of the time I was sad on the inside but kept a smile on the outside. This is what I had become accustomed to, my mom was the best teacher of moving through the pain. No matter how dark times may have been, she always kept a smile on her face with grace and beauty. It was an adjustment that I would experience throughout my teen years into adulthood. I'm not here to dehumanize my dad but to share a piece of my reality that I was ashamed of. My dad worked tirelessly and provided for his family. I longed for us to have a strong daddy/daughter bond and maybe he wanted that as well but just didn't know how to build on that.

My parents would separate and get back together throughout my childhood which kept me on an emotional roller coaster. Throughout my parents' marriage with all of the auguring, cursing, fighting, and separating on a consistent basis, they never collectively made the decision to get a divorce. I don't really think that they could possibly truly live without each other's presence no matter how toxic it sometimes was. They met and fell in love at an early age and the mental and physical connection was too heavy to let go.

My dad loved my mom but he also tap danced

with the demons and grief that were nestled in his spirit and drinking was his safe haven. When I was younger I never understood why she just wouldn't take her kids and leave him where he laid and part of me was angry at her for not leaving because I was tired of having to adjust to that environment. As I got older, and experienced a few relationships myself, I could relate to the connection of toxicity that she may have felt with my father. It may sound crazy but at times the toxicity felt good because it was the physical attraction that kept me there while it was destroying me emotionally.

Before my mom passed in 2016, when we weren't face to face we would talk on the phone for hours laughing, sharing thoughts and talking about the good ol' days. In one of our mother/daughters talks I was often curious and had questions about why she chose to stay with my dad and his drinking behavior. I always understood why she left when things got really bad, but for the life of me I didn't understand why she kept taking him back over and over and over again. When I one day asked her why, she replied, "I loved him." With those three words from her lips it was clear to me at that time no matter what my dad did or said that her heart was wrapped around his and she had no intentions to divorce him as long as they were alive.

There were good times in their marriage filled with laughter, singing and dancing. I know she hoped and prayed that he would get the help he needed for himself and I'd like to think that as much he loved my mother despite his faults, deep down in his heart, I know he wanted to get the help he needed but just didn't know how. What hurts my heart is that although I was able to see and experience some good times with them both, I'll never get to see and witness the healed parts of what their marriage could have been and to experience the best version of themselves.

The bitterness and anger I felt was taking over my spirit and I needed to be released from this dark cloud over me. I struggled for years suppressing and holding on to bitterness and anger of my childhood and adolescent years that it was festering and boiling in my gut. As a kid, I didn't quite understand what and why things were happening every time we had to uproot and move. As I got older the more times we left my dad and moved. I didn't know how to channel or address my anger and bitterness into positive energy.

In my days growing up you didn't talk about what was going on behind closed doors and how it made us feel. I was too embarrassed and ashamed to mention it to any of my peers at school so my bitterness, and anger would be deeply suppressed and I would just bear it and move on with my daily routine. In some instances it was easier for me to hold on to it because when negative things would happen in my life or my relationships would fail, I would resort to the blame game and use my past as an excuse for my failures instead of addressing the issue.

The longer I let it fester the more angry I felt and even depressed at times. I was very good at masking the pain and disappointment of what I was feeling and I would often imagine and dream about how different my life would be if my dad didn't drink, and if he and my mother embodied a wholesome and loving marriage how my thought process and views about relationships may have been different. I did not choose this life, it was given to me and I refuse to keep holding on to the anger and bitterness of what I experienced. I had to find a way to address my anger and bitterness and get a clear understanding as to why things happened in my life the way that it did. It was time to get answers to some unanswered questions about some of the turmoil in my childhood.

It wasn't until I got older as an adult, that I was ready to ask questions that I as a kid wanted to ask. That was the best and courageous decision that I made towards my healing to have an open mind and listening ears. The more questions I asked, the more answers I received, the more clearer my understanding was about why I was bitter and angry. I was more bitter and angry because I didn't understand about alcohol addiction and the triggers and the demons my dad was fighting within himself.

When I look back now, given what I know now about the significance of addressing anger and bitterness, I approach issues with different eyes. I am now more comfortable with talking and sharing about my feelings. I focus more on finding solutions to the problem rather than talking more about the problem.

When my dad passed in May 1991, I knew at that moment without my dad, I had to begin spreading my wings, stand up for myself, and take the lead in my life.

I was still holding on to the past hurt but it was too late to tell him that I was sorry and that I love him. I was struggling to forgive him because I didn't understand him or his upbringing. Later in my adulthood, I had begun to do some soul searching to free myself of this deep-rooted pain. I looked to my family and had some extensive conversations about my dad and his childhood/adulthood life experiences.

I had a clearer understanding and learned of painful events in his past that may have contributed to his abuse of alcohol. In 2014, I was finally freed from the anger and bitterness I felt toward my dad and was able to finally forgive him and restore my peace of mind that was taken away from me. I was proud of myself for taking that major step to forgive. Your

peace is more important than anything that makes

you mad. Allowing anger to fester and fuel up inside

of us, paves the way to sin. I focus on God and my

relationship with Him rather than the bad things that

I have experienced.

CHAPTER 3

Broken Wings

"Though tired and a little broken, her wings still carried her dreams" ~A.C. Sparks~

This will be my most vulnerable chapter and hardest to write in this book. It's not easy to express and recount the hurt and pain from my past, but the one thing I am learning and appreciating is being able to talk about and share your pain will help other people that share similar pain. After losing both my parents at a point in my life when I needed them the most, it was easier for me to give up on spreading my wings and die a butterfly in a jar. The more deeply I encounter hurt and pain the more isolated and quiet I become nestled in thought and even in tears. I could ponder for days – even weeks - on a situation, overthinking and constantly recounting the incidents leading to my hurt.

Have you ever been so deeply hurt by losing something or someone and in the midst of that hurt you start to blame yourself and ask those "what if" questions. 'What if I had been there? What if I had done more? ``"What if I had called more?" Focusing on the "what if's" caused me to fall into a state of depression because I couldn't climb out of the blame-shifting hole I created in my mind. I was feeling a bit insecure and apprehensive to move on without my parents, but the only thing I could depend on at this point in my life was FAITH. As Les Brown would say "there is greatness within you." I realized there is a beautiful world and exciting adventures beyond this jar I felt suffocated in.

I would have never imagined being parentless at the age of forty-five, when I lost both of my parents at different times of my life. My father Jesse, an Atlanta native, attended and graduated from the L.J Price High School. He was handsome and quiet most of the time, until he was "in his tea" as my mom would say (which meant his alcohol). He loved his family and music.

I would love to hear him sing those old R&B Souls hits and we even sang together sometimes. He would reflect and talk about the days when he was part of a singing group with some of his friends. Performing in talent shows in high school they even won against the worldwide group as we know today Glady's Knight and the Pips. They performed at small Atlanta nightclubs, and would practice with a local American vocal group from Atlanta called "The Tams". The group remained together for years but the indulgence of alcohol would be the demise to their rise to the top.

This part of my dad's life is a blur for me as I was too young to remember, but according to the conversation with my brother, all the members were friends who hung out together and love to sing together. They had all the characteristics vocally to be famous all over the world but with no manager, no coaching, no structure, and the demonic indulgence in alcohol was the ultimate demise of the group. The world will never know what legacy this group of talented voices could have been.

My dad had been employed with the Dairymen Inc since 1979 located in Atlanta, Georgia. The cool thing about my dad working for a milk company was when he brought home my favorite flavor chocolate milk and ice cream. My dad and I didn't have a lot of daddy/daughter moments but I cherished the ones we did have. He loved me and I loved him, I wished we had more time together to build a bond but we never got that chance because he was called home in May 1991. He died of alcoholism and was found dead in his apartment by my brother and mother three days later. I was twenty years old and seven months pregnant with my first son.

Before he passed he was excited and looking forward to the birth of his grandson. He even made an early prediction before my ultrasound that I would give birth to a son. Imagine that!! He already knew the sex of my unborn child and somehow I like to believe that the last beautiful moment I spent with him smiling and laughing, he had a premonition that he would have to leave me before I gave birth. His death was unexpected and words can't express the pain I felt that day and still carry. I needed so much for him to be there, hug me, and reassure me that no matter what everything would be okay.

That time never came and I knew at that moment that I had to begin spreading my wings and be the best that I could be for myself and for my son. My dad may have not made it to fame with his singing talents or expressed the love that to me that I was searching for because of fighting his alcohol demons, but he embodied a hardworking man that loved his family and did the best he could with what he had.

My mother, Margaret, an Atlanta native, graduated from Booker T. Washington High School. As an educator she dedicated 20+ years of service with the Atlanta public school system and retired in 2007. Throughout her years of service, she educated, nurtured, motivated, and inspired with a purpose.

I admired my mother because she was not afraid to spread her wings and let her voice be heard. She didn't just talk the talk she walked the walk. She taught me that when life shakes you, disappoints you, hurts you, and scares you, you fight with every fiber in your body not to give in and give up. Hold your head up high and keep it moving. Mom didn't care what people thought of her, and she was going to live her best life in her own way. Beautiful skin was her makeup and she taught me how to remain a queen of beauty when I felt ugly. She never met a stranger and everybody that crossed her path felt her genuine love, warm heart and her pretty smile was contagious.

From the moment I was born our mother/daughter bond was strong and still remains today. Mom desperately wanted a girl and when that moment came she didn't hesitate to show it by shopping every chance she got. Proud of her baby girl at an early age she would change my clothes a few times a day and prop me on the bed like a baby doll and look at me for hours. Hearing the stories from her before she passed and family members of how crazy in love she was over me just melts my heart.

I had everything a little girl could ask for and more. From clothes to toys and barrettes to bangs my mom gave me a head start in being quite the Little Diva. Now don't get me wrong... transitioning into a teen was problematic I must say. Like most teens, we think we know it all, start smelling ourselves and think that our parents are old fashioned. Let's just say my mom proved all of that wrong and then some. She didn't hesitate to let me know who was the real Queen Bee in the household. But as I got older and became a parent myself, I'd grown to appreciate and be thankful for her presence and her love even more.

We would talk on the phone for hours, go shopping together and yes, she would still shop for me from time to time. I'd like to think my mom admired me for the woman I'd become. Granted I've made some bad decisions and wrong choices but she never stopped loving me or supporting me. Now she didn't agree with some of my choices and expressed her concerns but she allowed me to learn and grow without judgement and I appreciated her for that. Time was moving on and she was getting older and her health started to decline due to years of smoking cigarettes. She was bound to a breathing machine for years but that feisty spirit was still there. In 2016, she was admitted to the hospital to receive extensive breathing treatment for pneumonia of the lungs. I didn't worry too much because she had been hospitalized for the same thing and recovered.

I never gave up hope and I prayed for God to heal her so she could return home to us. Her health went from bad to worse in a matter of weeks. I never would forget receiving that phone call in the middle of the night from the hospital saying, "hurry and get to the hospital because your Mom won't make it through the night." I sat on the side of the bed and gathered myself together to take that long drive to the hospital. The doctor told me that her heart stopped twice and that she had a massive heart attack. She was kept on a breathing machine until the family could get there to say our goodbyes. I didn't want to let her go but I knew that she didn't want to live the life of a vegetable either. The hardest decision in my life I'd ever had to make was removing her from the breathing machine and letting her go with GOD.

I reminisce on our mother/daughter bond and my best moment and memory was that she was with me and held me when I took my first breath and I was there with her, holding her hand as she took her last breath. Experiencing the loss of both my parents, my wings felt broken and bruised and sometimes I've felt that I couldn't recover. Both of my parents are deceased now! I would have loved for my parents to both be here in this moment and witness my acting and writing accomplishments. To look at the once scared little girl blossom into this RELENTLESS woman with more determination to be better and do better in the life I was given.

We all want to do something in our lives that our parents would be proud of. I wasn't born with a silver spoon in my mouth and neither was my parents.

I wanted them to see that no matter how dysfunctional our family was and how our lives were sometimes turned upside down that I rose above the ashes and flourished into somebody GREAT!

I can move forward knowing that my mom and dad have gained their angel wings and they are cheering and watching over me.

CHAPTER 4

Spreading my Wings

"As you spread your wings, you will go further than you could have ever imagined!"

Having to sit in the consequences of your actions will change your thought process, the way you view yourself internally and externally. Although my thought process started to change, however, I still felt like a butterfly in a jar. My mind was inflated with ideas, dreams, and goals, but my body felt like a block of cement. I knew there was a world of possibilities waiting to be released in my future.

When my sons were younger, they participated in the recreational sport of football which is one of the reasons why I love the sport. I enjoyed watching them play the game and being a team player with the other teammates. The days were long and it never seemed like there was enough time in the day between work, practice, homework, household chores and keeping my sanity intact. Grueling practices in the heat and cold, hard hits from tackles begin to take a toll on their bodies. Being the nurturing mom that I am, I couldn't sit back and watch them in pain.

With no previous massage therapy experience, my maternal instincts kicked in and I began to massage their aching muscles and light stretching. It seemed to work as the loud grunts began to silence with a mother's touch. I felt a sigh of relief and calmness that they were going to be okay. Days went by and I was still thinking about the choice I made to take action in a scary situation and chose massage therapy for the solution. It brought comfort and healing to my boys and in 2006, I decided to spread my wings and enroll into a massage therapy program to properly learn how to administer therapeutic care to my boys.

The thought of entering any school at this point of my life had not crossed my mind. I had previously enrolled in two colleges but never completed the programs. I was enrolling in schools with no vision and it was frustrating, again feeling like a Butterfly In a Jar. I had set my mind on going to college but never fulfilled it in its entirety. I enrolled twice at two different colleges and both times I withdrew because I was a kid frustrated and wasn't sure what I wanted to do, I was un-focused, I was tired of school, I felt like I was going in circles with no clue about my future. Feeling suffocated in a world where everyone expects you to follow the masses, I needed to exhale and figure things out on my own. As I look back, I think about if I had stuck it out how different my life could have been. My choices didn't change my desire for greatness, my choices changed my desire to be different.

Receiving my diploma in Massage Therapy gave me a purpose and excitement. This gave birth to Bodyflow Inc. Massage Therapy in 2007. Now I can feel my wings begin to spread and air began to slowly fill my determination to fly. I had been in a stagnated fear zone questioning myself and my abilities to soar when really what I was doing was doubting God's ability to equip and prepare me for the journey. After we release the contents of our hearts to God's ears, he will order your steps. I was forcing myself to stay stagnated in certain situations because it felt safe and familiar, not realizing that taking a chance and stepping into new and scary opportunities will undoubtedly set you free.

I wanted change.....I needed change......I craved change......I wanted to break free of the continuity of my life. I had swam the oceans of disappointments, drove through the valleys of heartaches, crossed the bridges of defeat. But through it all, I had relied on God and now I'm climbing the mountains of I WANT IT ALL. A woman's passport filled with trials and tribulations, soaring through the clouds like the Raven that I am, no uncommon boundaries will stop me. I've seen failure all too often mixing up this concoction of strength, motivation, determination, high expectations, my cup runneth over to the younger generation.

To spread this knowledge in rapid form, imaginations can be fulfilled as your body flows through time...time will reveal that your aim for success was never in question or in doubt. It was more like a natural high that elevates above the rest. Having a clear vision of my life's purpose and mission, under no condition will I be lead astray from my calling. Turning my pain into power, I have to remain grounded and focused for I know that my journey will be long and filled with adventures, opportunities, and life's mysteries to uncover within myself and in others.

Giving more than what is expected, feelings of neglect and rejection, I know this is a cover for my protection. Fear is a thing of the past, faith is in the palm of my hands, sowing the seeds that was planted in my soul from my life experiences and countless blessings. I ask no questions and let go and let GOD feed my spiritual appetite. Bite after bite I digest the importance of discernment, patience, power, and grace. Tears seldom stream down my face for I know I'm not alone in this race. I compete with no one, I answer to only one to lead me to my destiny, ordering my steps, my book has been written of this determined woman on a mission.....Priceless Queen...spreading her wings.

CHAPTER 5

Digest Yourself

"The secret of change is to focus all of your energy, not on fighting the old, but on building the new" ~Socrates~

In order to find yourself, you must first digest your past life experiences, ups and downs, imperfections, and recognize your strengths to elevate beyond your potential. When you can be true and embrace your unique self and not be ashamed of your past but rather appreciative of the lessons you become spiritually free. When you have a divine purpose set on your life that you can't control, you are destined for greatness for all the world to see. My divine purpose is to serve others, build relationships and create platforms for other people to come in and perfect their craft. To share my story, my life experiences and leave a lasting, impactful impression in the lives of people I touched.

What better way to do that, than by spreading your wings and taking control of the air quality in your life? You never know when your prayers will be answered but baby!!! Let me tell you, you best be prepared, Prepared?? You ask, but of course because opportunities will knock on your door and you have to be prepared to take the risk or lose the chance. 'When you stay ready, you don't have to get ready (one of my favorite quotes). There have been opportunities as I look back that I didn't take for fear of stepping into the unknown. I had prayed for opportunities but wasn't mentally prepared to take on the responsibilities.

One opportunity I didn't take because of fear was the opportunity to perform on stage in a one-person act. I submitted for the role online and was given the opportunity in the very beginning of my acting career. I had no onstage experience, I had only taken 2 acting classes and felt internally very inexperienced. I found myself constantly over thinking, constantly questioning and doubting myself. I would have rather buried my head in hot sand than to speak and/or perform at that time. Fearing that my voice would shake, I would stumble over my words or people wouldn't take me seriously would have been embarrassing. Replaying that over and over in my head, I hesitated too long and missed my first acting opportunity.

The pain of that missed opportunity because of fear angered me. It was up to me to stand up against the fear of performing in a large crowd. Who knows what great opportunities that could have been connected to my first time performing. I never wanted that feeling again or to compromise my career and professional development. I chose growth over comfort and fear when I realized everything I want is on the other side fear.

Seeing the poor- versus- broke mentality had me in a choke hold below sea level drowning in stinking thinking that my elevation and spreading my wings to the next dimension was far from reality, gasping for air so I closed my eyes and prayed to the highest one. Dear Lord, I come to you lost and broken, a mere token with the heart of gold and I long for answers to unfold. How can I achieve greatness? Without feeling weightless? In this late stage of my life? "Dear child of mine", he whispered, ("Trust in the Lord with all your heart and lean not on your own understanding. "(Proverbs 3:5)

The moment you convert your imaginations into intentions and your intentions into actions, a change will occur. Have faith over your fears, never shed a tear because Jesus said he will be with us all the days of our lives. I was overflowing with a layer of peace because the Lord heard my cry. With my head held high, I decided right then to change my attitude, pay it forward, and never look back. Mind over matter consciously and subconsciously I tell myself to keep pushing forward in all that I do and never let the

poor-versus-broke) mentality determine my altitude.

CHAPTER 6

FORGIVE YOURSELF

"The real difficulty is to overcome how you think about yourself" Maya Angelou.

Forgiving others has been a long hard road for me to travel but not as much as forgiving myself. Constantly inwardly shifting blame on myself about my failed marriage, parenting, relationships, friendships and making wrong choices was causing me to suffocate heavily as a butterfly in a jar. It didn't matter if it was my fault or someone else's, I was Intentionally overthinking a situation until it made sense and it didn't end well on my behalf. I felt drained, experiencing headaches, loss of appetite and insomnia.

I knew I could not move forward until I accepted the fact that some things cannot be explained and that it was unlikely that I would receive closure in every situation. Being honest about the events that happened in your life and releasing the negative energy will feel like a heavy burden that was lifted off your shoulders. When you can accept the unacceptable and come to terms with the fact that you cannot change the past, it will set you free and help you become the best version of yourself. When you decide that you want more in life and want to make some drastic changes in your life, you will experience God's test.

I can admit that I was a knucklehead and failed his test over and over again until I decided to take my time to learn the lesson and not avoid what the situation was telling me. You can't change what happened, but you can move forward by changing your attitude and actions in the present. Practice self-compassion, be kinder to yourself and commit to talking with yourself in ways that will be helpful and not harmful. As a parent we want to protect and care for our children and set an example for them to lead. I made the choice every day to put their happiness and wellbeing ahead of mine, to do the right thing, to teach the hard lessons even when I wasn't sure what the right thing was. Well, I'm no perfect patty and I didn't allow myself to admit that I wasn't a supermom and that I didn't always have it together and some of the decisions and/or choices I made affected my children's lives.. By doing that, as a parent, I had to forgive myself for not knowing what I didn't know before I learned it.

My life is more at peace with a purpose focusing on the good and truths about myself, rather than making my life a living hell drowning in toxic thoughts or situations. Nowadays, I focus on building my relationship with God rather than focusing on the wrong I've done or the wrong that was done to me. Forgiveness may be a hard pill to swallow but saying YES to the stretch will expand your vision and open your heart to new horizons. The distance between your comfort zone and oneself requires a bold stretch.

It will take you where you want to go and allow you to
be who you want to be without any distractions taking
drastic measures to complete any tasks. You are your
own #Brand You deserve the life you have visualized
and dreamed of. Forgive yourself for what you didn't
know, love yourself abundantly, spread your wings
and soar.

CHAPTER 7

LOVE YOURSELF

"Sometimes you have to love yourself

through the hurt in order to heal yourself"

Like I mentioned earlier, be prepared for what you pray for. The unexpected will arise when you least expect it. It's imperative to love yourself enough to know that you deserve everything life has to offer even after your past mistakes. But also love yourself just as much to not be passive and take disrespect from people. By my teenage/adolescent years, I had fallen into an identity crisis within myself. I grew up in predominantly black surroundings but my facial features were of a native American/Caucasian with small lips and pointed nose and a southern dialect.

I would get teased about this all the time and how I wasn't black enough because of my features. It used to hurt my feelings, but I would pretend it didn't. And for a brief moment I started to wonder "is there something wrong with me?" (notice I said a brief moment) When I looked in the mirror, I saw a beautiful black girl, but the outside saw me as different. My Aunt Gerry said to me once Kim, there was something special about you, you always were different and unique. My Aunt Gerry was right and I started to embrace and accept my beautiful unique self. It's not about what people say about you, it's about what you answer to and what you believe about yourself.

I looked in the mirror every day and fell in love with my different features and southern dialect. I accepted that this is the way GOD made me because I am fearfully and wonderfully made. No longer would I accept other people's perception of me. Beauty isn't just about how you look on the outside, it's about the way you treat people, the way you love, and the way you accept yourself. The love you show yourself will influence the way people will love you. Not everyone is going to love what you say and do but they will have to respect it. Loving myself was easy and I was getting more comfortable in my own skin. Wanting to be loved and getting it was a struggle for me. After my dad passed away I was searching for the love that I longed from him.

I was hurting deeply but didn't know how to express it verbally so the only way I knew how to cope was to suppress it without talking about it. It would seem real if I kept reminiscing on it. It was bad enough that I didn't get a chance to say goodbye but to visualize him lying on the floor while his body deteriorated was too much. By this time, my son had been born and my body was snatched back to my high school weight. I started to hang out and getting the attention of men was my medicine for my depression. I think back and realize instead of me entertaining men and relationships, I should have loved myself enough to seek the help I needed to cope with my depression. The need to feed my flesh of lust and love rather than feed my spiritual soul for healing was my biggest mistake in searching for that male presence.

What I thought at times was a connection for love, it was only a connection through similar past experiences and trauma. No healing process had taken place and trying to love over pain ended in disappointments. A repetitive amount of hurt will eventually take a toll on you, which will undoubtedly produce change. I was searching for love in all the wrong faces instead of looking in the mirror and loving myself. I had to drop my ego and pride and ask GOD to give me strength in my weak moments.

When I flip the script and start to focus more on feeding my soul and starving my flesh things miraculously started to change within me. I was a broken woman that was determined to rebuild herself with the stones that she was given. I had to die a little on the inside in order to rise again stronger and wiser.

The more you endure hurt, pain and disappointments it triggers something within your mindset and you begin to cry out for help. At times I was too ashamed to talk about anything that concerned me or what I was feeling. I would have rather kept things inside and painted this façade of having it all together.

Because I wanted to love and be loved deeply I disrespected my own self in situations and decisions I made. I felt my self-respect drowning in my BS and I knew my parents wouldn't want this kind of life for me, and I definitely didn't want my boys to lose respect for me. I love them more than anything in this world and it was high time that I started to love myself just as much. It's never too late to start anew and live a life I could be proud of.

I couldn't go back and change my beginning, but I changed my vision so I changed my ending. The things I used to tolerate were now intolerable. Where

I used to once remain silent, I am now speaking my truth. I am now beginning to understand and appreciate the value of my voice. Love yourself and realize that there are certain situations, people, places, and things that no longer deserve your energy, time, and focus. Let it go and glow in your growth.

CHAPTER 8

REINVENT YOURSELF

"If you want to reinvent yourself, focus on what you want and not on what you fear."

When the world says, "give up!" hope whispers "try one more time." And suddenly you'll know it's time to start something new and trust the magic of new beginnings. In the same way the caterpillar stops eating when they are full grown and becomes a pupa. The pupa may suspend under a branch, hidden in leaves or buried underground sometimes, for weeks, a month, or even longer. It may look like nothing is going on but big changes are happening on the inside.

I have created an unstoppable courageous woman with a strong measure in faith. I'm determined NOW more than ever to be successful, not just for me but to leave a legacy. When you're pushed to the limit and your back is up against the wall, choose the power to alter the direction of your life that allows you to reinvent yourself, change your future and that can powerfully influence the rest of creation. After the passing of my mother, I started to look at how I was living my life. I didn't view life the same and part of me actually had taken it for granted. Once the phone stopped ringing, friends and family condolences faded in the wind, it was time for me to return back to my place of employment. My mom had worked twenty plus years for the school system and didn't even live ten years after her retirement to enjoy it.

Thinking about that constantly played in my mind and I can admit that it angered me and I knew at that moment, I didn't want to live my life that way. To work for a company tirelessly, for 20+ years, retire and then die with the unfilled dreams. We look at our age, our financial status and if we're in pretty good shape, we think we'll live forever. I knew that wasn't possible and I refused to be stagnant until my death. I wanted to live life more abundantly and exist on my own terms. Like most teens, I started working at the age of 16 just to earn money and buy things. I became a mom at the age of 19, when I should have been in the college of my choice to evolve in my track and field career. Nevertheless, I chose the responsibility of being a mom taking care of my parental responsibilities.

By the age of twenty-five, I was married and by the age of twenty-nine, I was a divorced single mom raising two boys. My marriage failed because the both of us were carrying the mental weight and suppressing past experiences and unhealed wounds. I was focused more on my external happiness, taking care of family/kids, and spent little to no time working on my internal pain and issues. I was very good at living a life outside of my pain all the while the pain inside that was in the pit of my stomach ached to be healed.

As I look back on my marriage we were two imperfect people trying to love each other over our pain. Until I heal myself as a woman, the love we shared was never going to be enough. Just as we shared in loving each other, we also caused pain to one another as well. I'm going to be brutally honest with this statement "If I knew then, what I know now, I never wouldn't have gotten married because I wasn't ready for marriage mentally, spiritually or emotionally at the age of 25. I have no regrets about being married. My only regret was that I didn't love myself enough before I said, "I DO". I wasn't the perfect spouse and it has taken me years and a lot of work internally and spiritually to mature psychologically, allow myself to heal, and to love myself wholeheartedly again.

I never gave up on the idea of taking a risk and living life on my terms. As I watched my sons grow from boys to men, I could finally sit back, exhale and ask myself "what do I want to do now?" Or more importantly "what do I want to be?" All my life I've been taking care of others and putting my dreams, ideas, and goals on hold. But enough was enough!! It was my time and the time was now!! I had been employed with the county government for thirteen years and made the decision to step out on faith, resign and focus solely on my massage therapy business full-time.

It was a decision and risk that had been on my mind and in my heart for some time. I took the time to plan and execute. When the time and moment arose, I walked out the doors in 2018 into entrepreneurship. I quickly dove into my new adventure reinventing myself as a full-time massage therapist and didn't look back. I believed in myself enough to lean heavily on God because He was all I had and needed. I wouldn't be honest if I didn't admit that at times I was a little scared, apprehensive, and doubting myself, but you know what? Through all the tears, failures, and mistakes, I bit the bullet and learned from my mistakes. It's at the time when you're at the bottom and feel buried in a hole that you find a way to dig yourself out of the pit of hell and re-strategize the process. I kept high-stepping and adjusting my mindset to keep moving.

I couldn't have made it through without prayer, motivational videos, reading and writing in my prayer journal daily. When you're in the process of reinventing yourself you have to be willing to shed your dead skin of your old self, friendships, relationships, and things that fog your focus. I felt suffocated and stagnated with my everyday lifestyle. At any moment, your life can change and your steps can be redirected. I was so engulfed and focused on my massage therapy practice working on clients restoring their peace of mind that at times I was losing mine. What I didn't expect was God to shift my focus and redirect my steps in an instant to a venture with no previous experience.

In 2017, I decided to audit an acting class at The Alliance Theater. My expectations were to watch and observe but the instructor had a different agenda. I was asked to participate in a humorous skit performing as 'Madea". Hey, I'm no professional but did the best I could. She) obviously was pleased as she asked after class had I ever thought about acting. I replied, "no not at all", her response was "well you should really consider it." I left thinking WOW!! Maybe I do have something to offer and present to the acting arena. I know it could be challenging, hardcore and cutthroat. But I also know that it could be rewarding, successful and life changing. That's it!

That's what I was looking to do, to keep evolving and elevating into the next dimension. I've always been intrigued with the actors and actresses I saw on TV and the different characters, body language and gestures they would display. I didn't see myself on TV, although I could imitate characters and memorize lines to a T. When I would do impressions of characters, people around me would laugh and say, "do it again" or "girl you should be on TV". I would brush it off because of the fear I had of performing and speaking in front of an audience. I had to have some real inner conversations with myself and my fcars.

The only way to conquer this fear was to address it head on. I can honestly say that the more I thought about it the more excited and curious I became. The time and opportunity came for me to give it a try and find out what the acting industry entails. I enrolled in class in 2018 and have been flourishing as an actor in film, TV, movies, and music videos. I'm most proud of myself for conquering the fear of performing and speaking in front of an audience.

Sitting in class, taking notes, asking questions, and reenacting scenes from various playwrights and/or film was so surreal. Reinventing myself from entrepreneur to actress was and is hard work. I committed to staying in classes every chance that was presented and learning under the direction of several other instructors. I had been bitten by the acting bug and it was not covering this up with a band-aid. Walking into unfamiliar territory alone can be scary but shifting your attitude comes from your belief system and it produces confidence. Finding your role and playing it under authority you've been placed gives you pleasure and purpose.

There is no passion in playing it small and I wanted to be taken serious as an actress. I was on a mission to leave a legacy and manifest my gift. As the saying goes "your gift will make room for you" The right seed had been planted in the right moment and God was calling me into my authenticity. I was eager to learn and was prepared for my life's blueprint and took the initiative to submit for background roles to get a closer hands-on experience at how film production works. Background and/or non-speaking roles come with long hours and little to no pay.

The onset experience was just the push I needed to readjust my flight course as an actress. I believed in myself fully enough to submit for speaking roles. My determination to achieve greatness was enlightened by faith. I mentioned in an earlier chapter be prepared for what you pray for. I received my first speaking role in the stage play "Front Porch Society" as the nosey neighbor 'Winnie". Dominating that role not only gave me confidence to continue to submit for other speaking roles but it reinvented and fueled my self-confidence and a new self-discovery about myself. Since then, my roles and debuts can be seen in music videos, television, radio, and films. When you believe in yourself and can adjust to the process, you will be able to master anything and can reinvent yourself into what and who you were meant to be.

CHAPTER 9

PRAYER AND PREPARATION

"Prepare prayerfully, Plan purposefully,

Proceed Positively, Pursue Persistently"

~Myles Munroe~

The year 2020 has definitely proved to be one of the most stressful and unpredictable years in my lifetime to date. Leaving 2019 with positive vibes and an optimistic outlook on what was to come, I was excited to continue my success as an entrepreneur and my newfound love as an actress. My butterfly wings were finally starting to spread and I could feel the fresh air filling my lungs. Starting the new year off on a new spiritual path, I was baptized and recommitted my life back to Christ and became a member of Now Faith Apostolic Ministries.

I was baptized at a very young age and attended church and bible study on a regular basis but didn't quite understand or fully comprehend the Word of God and His plans for me. As I got older I was living in the moments of life and straying further away from God by partying on a consistent basis, fornicating in relationships, twisted up in the latest gossip and drama. My children were now adults and living their own lives, both my parents were deceased and I fell into a slump of depression, and when I looked back on my life all I saw was a resume full of work experiences and not a boldness of career driven. My life just seems to be going in circles without internal happiness, peace, and fulfillment. When you are living your best life without structure and a plan it can be disastrous and have you living in a downward spiral.

I wanted my life to change and I knew I couldn't do it by myself. It was time for a major soul shift. I thought about changing all the time but hesitated on taking the first step because I still craved the savageness of society and being in the limelight. Even while living reckless God always kept his hands on me with his mercy and grace. He loved me when I didn't love myself. He kept me safe from harm. He saved me from self-destruction. He has given me second chances over and over and over again. I can't repay GOD enough for what he has done for me and watched over me so I decided the best thing for me to help myself was to renew and strengthen my relationship with God and be transformed of mind, body and spirit and I gave my life back over to God in 2020. This decision has changed the way I view life because when things started to change within me, things started to change around me.

I was able to look in the mirror and not only like what I saw but loved what I saw. It all starts with how you see yourself and what areas in your life that need to be renewed and restored. I saw myself doing more, being more, loving more, dreaming more, planning more, succeeding more. I didn't want to miss out on the abundance of blessings and His purpose God has for my life. Releasing the toxicity and negativity in your life will free you from a decaying spirit and will connect you to your destiny and future. I am more than a conqueror and my comeback will always be stronger than my setbacks.

I wanted to be a life coach to help facilitate growth and change of mind, body, and spirit. I'm familiar with the challenge of having to pick yourself up out of the pits of life, weapons of rejection, fear, and setbacks. This may have been my strength but it's also a weakness in others. Becoming a life coach provided an opportunity for me to create a partnership in the lives of others and to help them take back their power, find inner peace and freedom, reveal, and attract their desires, set goals, and get the results in their lives, careers, business, and organizations.

I've always enjoyed inspiring and helping people and took my education a step further and earned a diploma as a Certified Life Coach from the Georgia Certified Life Coaching Academy. The month of January had my soul on fire from the outpouring of blessings. I was high stepping in favor and grace and in February I celebrated my 49th birthday. Even at the highest peak of celebratory status at the blink of an eye things can change dramatically. Who would have thought that the year 2020 would bring raging bushfires, police brutality reaching a boiling point and the worst pandemic in recent history.

No one expected to experience a mandated lockdown, massive loss of jobs and businesses, and unemployment at an all-time high. This had proved to be a mass destruction not just in the USA but across the world and it created a state of shock and uncertainty. Not being able to visit friends and family and having your entire life come to a sudden halt was unbearable at times. During the first months of the pandemic, I felt at times like pulling my hair out and screaming to the top of my lungs. I was on edge and had cabin fever to the point if I left home I wouldn't come back.

While the world was in an emotional and dysfunctional state I knew I had to shift my entire thought process to something positive. I was fortunate to have friends and family that I could reach out to and talk via a phone call, text messages and on our social media platforms to make sure that everyone was okay or at least doing the best that they could. Anytime I felt overwhelmed, and needed to exhale, I would go and sit in a lounge chair in my backyard to think and strategize. Let's face it, we had plenty of time on our hands for days, weeks and months due to the nationwide lockdown. I began to pray more, read my bible, and write in my journal daily. The expectancy from the government and this pandemic will have you doubting and place the worst fears in your heart.

I refuse to sit back and wait in fear. I had come too far to stop believing in myself or my brand. When you want to be successful as much as you want to breathe, then you'll be successful. My goal is to not only be successful but to leave a legacy and I couldn't do that if I was constantly focused on foolishness. Once my thought process changed, I could finally see the light at the end of a tunnel. I woke up with a purpose, prayed and prepared to accomplish my daily goals.

Don't let what goes on around you change what's in you. If you crave elevation then prepare yourself for isolation to get yourself together. There was a fire of determination burning within me and the flames were getting intense. Have you ever heard the voice of God but you ignored it to do things your way?

Yeah me too, and it was a disaster. BUT the moment I let go and let GOD take control, I started living in a place of peace. In the midst of my storm I found me and I fell in love with me all over again. Prayer definitely changes things and prepares you for what God has for you.

CHAPTER 10

R.E.LE.N.T.L.E.S. S

"It's about being fearlessly, relentlessly and true to yourself as you spread your butterfly wings"

This is the last stage in the process of me transitioning from a caterpillar to the butterfly in a jar who is now ready to spread her pretty purple wings and fly. Your relentless mindset is what separates the best from the rest. I cannot stress this enough to others or get it out of my mind. Don't be afraid to stand out from the crowd and create your own lane. Growing up I always felt different and unique. I wasn't comfortable with being stagnant, or being controlled by people, places, or things. I wanted to utilize my creativity to overflow in my gifts.

All things are possible when you believe in your ideas, dreams, and goals. Throughout my life span there have been loves loss, obstacles, storms, and bumps in the road that tried to detour me and even stop me on the tracks of progression. Suffering from the many losses in my life, it seems only natural to give up on the belief that I could be somebody that makes a difference in the lives of others and the world. I became relentless in doing well and set my sights on the future because I had the crazy faith and belief that everything was working out for my good. My steps had already been ordered and it was up to me to be dedicated and passionate in pursuit of my happiness and goals.

I wasn't happy all the time or satisfied with the outcomes, decisions, and choices but my relentless attitude allowed me to push through to keep going. Get comfortable with being uncomfortable when you are elevating to a new dimension. Understand that you will not always have a support team, everybody won't understand and see your vision, and that some relationships and/or friendships have taken its course and run out of time and you must depart from them. When God removes what you thought you wanted or needed, don't fight the feeling, and just know that He will replace it with something better beyond what you can imagine. My thirst for greatness was quenching everyday with the need to stay the course.

When I stumbled, I regained my focus, when I fell, I got back up, when I was tired, I rested but I never gave up. I saw my future and it was clear and bright and full of happiness. I wanted to be a part of that and was ambitious enough to get it. So I kept praying and preparing in spite of what was happening around me because I'm in the world but not of it. I was about to take the world by storm in my acting career and other endeavors. Be relentless in your assignment and be driven with purpose.

Discount and pay no attention to the disimpassioned haters. You are more than enough to breed success and achieve everything within your world of influence. Recognize that you are the prize and begin to put everything in motion to reach that mountain. I woke up with a relentless attitude every day and set my expectations high to accomplish what I set out to do. Be open to adjust when things don't go as planned and navigate to higher grounds. The process won't be pretty but it is critical to finish what you start. You have so many things to be grateful for, find and fixate your vision on that.

During this pandemic, I engaged in conversation with friends, family, colleagues and on a radio show. The first question that always started the conversation was how are you holding up during this pandemic? my response every time was prayer and preparation. It was an unexpected eye-opening response. Manifesting in those two, I discovered something magical and deep within myself that wasn't there before. My life cycle was running parallel with the butterfly process. Through all those obstacles and in time of isolation, God was testing, transitioning, positioning, redefining, and preparing this Butterfly in a Jar to spread her wings and fly

R.E.L.E.N.T.L.E.S.S.L.Y

About the Author

Kimberly "Mz. Hollywood" Raven

Kimberly Raven born and raised Georgia Peach, is a professional actor in the Atlanta area. She began her career by studying at the Alliance Theatre, New African Grove Theater, Evolve Acting Studios, West End Performing Arts Center and Georgia Media Academy. Kimberly made her theatrical debut in the play **"Front Porch Society"** as the nosey neighbor "Winnie." She has also branched out into television as a main character in the YouTube web series **"Bad Practice"** as the no-nonsense "Vivian" Kimberly is currently working on the production of Wellspring **the movie** as (Karen Wolf) in **Sista Girls** as (Renee) Marvelous **the movie** as (Lottie) **In Memory Of** as (Mrs. Jones) in **Black Love Future series** as (Adele) in YOU as (Sa'ida) in The **Curse Within** as (Jackie Taylor). Kimberly has made her featured debut in the Lifetime movie **You Can't Take My Daughter** and in Barry Jenkins **Underground Railroad**. In addition to acting, she has augmented her acting skills by working in production as a production assistant, casting assistant, and producer. Kimberly has added to her accolades narrator for audiobooks and completed her first audio book "My Father Poisoned Me" now on AMAZON PRIME. Kimberly is the mother of two adult sons and enjoys bowling, fitness, and cheering for her Atlanta Falcons. Kimberly has been a Licensed Massage Therapist since 2007 and is the owner of BodyFlow Inc Massage Therapy, In January 2020 she received her diploma as a Certified Life Coach and is the owner of Goals 2 Results Life Coaching. In 2021 Kimberly signed with East Coast Talent Agency and looks forward to excelling in her acting career. What sets me apart not only in my personal life but in my business career is that I wake up with a R.E.L.E.N.T.L.E.S.S attitude and set my expectations high to accomplish what I set out to do. I'm not afraid to stand out from the crowd, create my own lane and be purpose driven. Manifesting in "prayer" and "preparation" I discovered something magical and deep within myself that wasn't there before. The process of success isn't easy and giving up isn't an option for me. The best thing I ever did was believe in ME!! I'm destined for greatness and I'm more determined now to make it.. I would like to leave my readers with this motivational nugget. Be relentless in your assignment and remain open to learn, listen, grow, communicate, let go, forgive, be coachable, be transparent, read motivational books, listen to motivational speakers, and adjust your mindset when life calls for a change.

Music Video debuts: Better Days music video with Mope Williams from WildnOut and Kendrick of the South Video with Jordan Carter

Contact me at: bodyflowinc@gmail.com

Facebook: Kimberly Raven

Linked IN: Kimberly Raven

Instagram: Mz_Hollywood41

Movies now showing on Amazon Prime.

Sista Girls

Wellspring

Underground Railroad

You Can't Take My Daughter